How to Grow  Small Space from Start to Finish

Simple and Easy - Anyone can do it!

Copyright © 2016

ISBN-13: 978-1537300153
ISBN-10: 1537300156

Table of Contents

1. About the plant..1
   Marijuana life cycle 1
   Male and Female 2

2. Shopping List...4
   Seeds 4
   Grow Tent 5
   Lights 6
   Odor control 6

3. The Process...7
   Ordering seeds...7
   Soil 9
   Containers 10
   Germination and Seeding 13
   Pre-flowering 17
   Flowering stage 18
   Harvest time 20
   Example of a growing process...............................23

4. Plant health...28
   Pest control...28
   Fertilizing 31
   Watering 33
   Controlling temperature 36
   Using Artificial lights 37
   Light reflection 43
   Ventilation 45

5. Extra 47
Hiding your plants from the outside world 47
Cloning your marijuana plants 50
Final words 52

1. About the plant

Growing marijuana indoors has many benefits as compared to growing it outdoors. Apart from hiding the plant from the authorities or from being stolen, most people prefer growing it indoors to control the environmental conditions such as CO2, humidity, temperature and lighting levels as the plant grows through different stages.

Marijuana life cycle

The life cycle of the marijuana plant starts with the seeds which are commonly produced by the male and female plants. However, there are some rare moments where these seeds are produced by a single hermaphrodite plant.

After the seeds are produced, they have the capacity to endure the test of time and can stay for a very long time provided they're exposed to the right temperatures and kept in a cool dark place. Once they're exposed to light, heat and water, cannabis seeds immediately sprout and commence the germination process.

lemon kush day 81

Germination is usually the second stage after your seeds are exposed to moisture and light. In this process, the plant cuts through the shell to start germinating. This stage is usually characterized by two cotyledon leaves appearing just above the soil.

After a week of initial growth, the seeding stage begins. Here, you'll notice the original leaves of the marijuana plant developing. The rooting system becomes steadier while the production of chlorophyll will become paramount from this point on. The seeding stage usually lasts for 3--6 weeks.

The vegetative stage is the next process which is usually very paramount in the marijuana life cycle. At this point, the plant takes its original shape and grows as fast as 2 inches per day. At this stage, your marijuana plant is capable of absorbing more nutrients from the soil and becomes more responsive to light. The plant becomes healthier when grown indoors as compared to outdoors as you're able to manipulate the light pattern even at night.

The last stage of the marijuana life cycle is the flowering stage. At this point, your plant is mature enough to reproduce. Also remember that, at the end of the vegetative stage, the marijuana is easy to distinguish between a male and a female. At the flowering stage, resin is also visible on the surface of the leaves and buds. The resin contains an active ingredient called THC. Once the THC has achieved its highest level, the plant is ready for harvest.

Male and Female

Did you know that there are male and female marijuana plants? Yes, this is actually one of the most fundamental aspects a farmer should consider. Note that, it's usually impossible to tell the gender of your cannabis plant until it reaches the vegetative and the flowering stage. During the vegetative stage (childhood stage), the plant only focuses on growing bigger and taller. Towards the end of this stage, a farmer might notice some signs which can tell whether the cannabis plant is male or female.

During the flowering stage (when the plant is 6 weeks old), a farmer can easily tell the sex of the cannabis plant. Usually at this stage, the cannabis plant has grown big and is only focusing on developing its generation. The female plant usually takes longer to show their first signs than the male. However, after they're fully grown, they develop the pistil and focus on flowering the entire plant. On the other hand, the male marijuana plant develops the generation at an early stage. The male doesn't flower and after some time, the buds bursts open and spills pollen grains everywhere.

Male cannabis plant

When growing cannabis plants, the female plants are the only once that produce flowers/buds that contain the right amounts of THC. The male only produce pollen which fertilizes the female. Now, if the female is fertilized, it will focus more on producing seeds than buds. Therefore, it's important to eliminate any male marijuana strain in your garden and only focus on the female if you're looking forward to grow marijuana.

2. Shopping List

Growing cannabis at home may not turn as easy as people may think it is. Although the final product may cost just a few bucks in the black market, it's sad to say that this inflated cost is not even close to the actual cost of growing this plant. Therefore, to maximize profits when growing and selling cannabis, this section will review some of the fundamental factors you'll need to consider before starting off.

Seeds

The best cannabis seeds to consider when growing marijuana are those sold by approved seed companies. Research on the best strains which are capable of performing well in your grow room. Unless you're planning on breeding your cannabis, always buy feminized seeds as they're the ones that produce the required amounts of THC.

This is how marijuana seeds looks like

Grow Tent

The size of your tent or grow area is one of the key factors you'll need to consider when growing marijuana for the first time. Depending with the quantity of your strains, you may either set up a small or a large grow tent. Since some species of the cannabis may end up being tall or broad depending with the lighting, temperatures and fertilizers used, your grow room should have either of these measurements; 1m (H)×0.75m (W)×1m (L) or 3ft (H)×3ft (W)×5ft (L).

Typical grow tent with grow light, ventilation and reflection (more on this in later chapters)

Lights

The amount of light exposed to your marijuana directly impacts the amount of THC you'll harvest. In the past, marijuana farmers relied on High Intensity Discharge lights such as Metal Halide systems and High Pressure Sodium lights to grow marijuana on its different growth cycles. However, due to their high wattage and increasingly hot characteristics, these lights consume a lot of electricity and require a grower to install carbon filters and extraction fans for perfect air conditioning. Due to this reason, marijuana growers have been forced to advance to the latest LED lights which are energy efficient, durable and easy to operate.

Odor control

A cannabis plant doesn't produce any odor until it gets to the flowering stage. At such a point-- depending with the location of your grow room/tent as well as the number of strains you're growing—you may either decide to install a carbon filter or an air extraction unit. However, in case you're growing small strains for your own personal use, consider purchasing an Ona Block Pro. Depending with the amount of smell in your room, opening the lid of the container for some time will neutralize the cannabis odor in your room.

Odor control is important when you grow indoors

3. The Process

The process of growing cannabis is not as easy as some people may think. Most farmers willing to grow this plant have made a lot of mistakes along the line which have resulted in poor yields in the long run. Cannabis plants can live in any environment and can easily adapt to different climates throughout the world. The female cannabis plant is usually the one responsible for producing flowers and buds which make up the final product.

Cannabis plant usually goes through a long process before its harvested. For a period of four months, the plant goes through the seeding stage, germination, pre-flowering, flowering and finally the harvesting stage. After it's harvested, the buds are dried and can either be smoked, eaten, vaporized or used for medicinal purposes. In this chapter, we will walk through the entire process a marijuana plant goes through before it's harvested and consumed.

Ordering seeds

Whether you're an experienced cannabis farmer or if you're not, ordering the best seeds is paramount. With the right seeds, the rate of germination will be exceptionally high and you'll not experience many complications during growth. While some farmers will opt to purchase cheap seeds, wise farmers will suggest buying high quality seeds which will deliver higher yields in the long run.

There are some important factors you need to keep in mind when ordering marijuana seeds. Firstly, you need to recognize where exactly you're planning to grow your seeds. Some people may prefer outdoor farming while others may prefer growing the plants indoors.

There are other things you need to keep in mind when ordering your cannabis seeds. What's the estimated flowering period? What's the THC content of the marijuana once it's fully grown? And is it auto-flowering? Since this guide is aimed at enlightening those new farmers who want to know more about the life cycle of the marijuana, we will review some of the best marijuana seeds available in the market.

Before we commence, let me point out that marijuana seeds can be ordered either online or from trusted outlet stores. Note that, depending with your needs, you can opt to order female seeds which will produce more buds and deliver greater results than a mix of male and female seeds.

With that being said, let's review some of the best marijuana seeds available in the market.

- **Purple Kush**: Purple Kush seeds are very easy to grow both indoors or outdoors. The final plant has high THC levels of 25% and is among the strongest marijuana with the fastest effects in the world when consumed. In the world of medicine, the Purple Kush is an effective treatment for depression, muscle spasms, insomnia and anxiety.

- **Girl Scout Cookies:** the seeds of the GSC are easy to find online and can grow in almost any climate throughout the world. The final plant has a THC of 22% and the flavor produced during consumption resembles that of cookies. In the world of medicine, this particular plant can cure stress, pain, nausea and depression.

- **White Widow**: if you ask any cannabis farmer out there, they'll tell you that the White Widow seeds are among the best in the market. The reason why they're referred to as White Widow is due to their white trichome crystals that develop at the final flowering stage of their cycle. The final plant has a magnificent 26% THC level which makes this plant the best for professional smokers and not beginners.

The white widow plant

Soil

After choosing the best quality seeds, the next prime concern is the soil. Professional cannabis farmers may opt to use hydroponics for pest control and to ensure that the plant gets enough nutrients for its growth. Since hydroponics is quite expensive to use, most farmers prefer the traditional method of using soil. Note that, using unsterilized soil may lead to high levels of parasites which may damage your cannabis at its initial stages. It's therefore important that you order quality soil from outlet stores, grocery stores or specialized gardening stores.

Other than spending a lot of bucks buying soil, you can opt to make your own soil mixture. Here's a short recipe you can rely on.

Mix moss, sand and sponge rock at the ratio of 2:1:1. Test the Ph level of your soil using a litmus paper or a soil testing kit. If the Ph needs to be raised, add a ½ lb of lime to a cubic foot of soil. If the Ph is too high, you can add chalk to lower it. If you insist on using the normal soil from your garden, it's important that you sterilize it. You can do this by moistening the soil then burning it at high temperatures of about 250°F for about an hour. Soil sterilization is very important for indoor cannabis farming as it ensures the safety of your plants as they undergo the growth cycle. This might not be worth the effort doing this, but we wanted to make a point that using soil from your garden is not a good idea.

As we wind up with this part, it's very important that you understand the fundamental properties that make up the best soil for growing healthy marijuana.

- The best soil should drain well. That means, it should contain a mix of sand, pearlite and sponge-rock.

- The soil should have a Ph level of between 6.5 and 7.5. This is because marijuana plants normally don't do well on acidic soils. Secondly, exposing the plant to acidic soils transforms it to a male making it less fertile.

- Finally, the soil should contain enough humus capable of retaining moisture and nutrients.

To test the Ph level of your soil you can get a Ph soil tester.

Containers

After you've prepared the soil, the next stage is to come up with containers to plant your cannabis in. Which are the best containers to use? Why are some containers better than others? These are some of the prime questions which most indoors farmers ask themselves. Among the best containers you can rely on when planting cannabis indoors include; smart pots, air-pots, hydro and hempy buckets.

- **Smart pots**: if you decide on using smart pots, consider using a pot twice as large as a normal container. This is because smart pots tend to lose water much faster meaning you'll have to water your cannabis plants more often.

- **Air pots**: these types of containers provide more oxygen to the roots and prevent your cannabis plants from getting root bound from the sides. Air pots contain large drainage holes on the sides which prevents you from overwatering your cannabis.

- **Hempy buckets**: these containers are large and the best for transplanting fully grown cannabis plants. Instead of having the drainage holes at the bottom, these containers' drainage holes are located on the sides near the bottom. After watering, small amounts of water are left at the bottom making it an advantage as you don't need to water the plant more often. These buckets are ideal for growing mature plants which need a lot of water to flower.

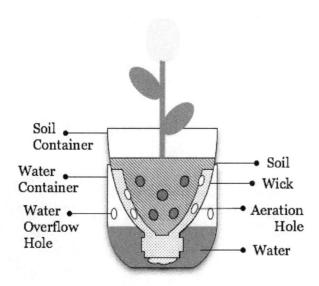

Example of the popular hempy bucket

Which containers should a cannabis farmer start with?

During the initial stages of your cannabis plant, it's wise to start with a small container usually 1 gallon. This is because, a small container dries much faster preventing chances of overwatering. Secondly, a small container delivers more oxygen to the roots of your cannabis accelerating the growth rate.

Note that, you should avoid planting your cannabis more than once as this can shock the plant and delay the growth rate. Always remember to fill the next container with soil then drill a small hole where the plant will fit in. When transplanting, scoop the small plant slowly without disturbing the root system. Always remember that for a cannabis plant to grow faster, the roots require;

- To be moist at all times. This is achieved by watering the plant more frequently.

- Enough oxygen at all times. This is achieved by using well drained soil and planting your strains in the right container.

- Enough nutrients for an accelerated growth. Your marijuana plant uses its roots system to deliver nutrients throughout the plant to flower and to make buds.

Common sight in a grow room

Germination and Seeding

The germination stage of a cannabis plant is very paramount. This stage requires a lot of care as it determines how healthy or how weak your plant will be in the future. The species of the marijuana plant originate from semi-arid and temperate areas. That means, the plant requires a lot of light, high temperatures and moderate amounts of water to grow. Therefore, when growing cannabis indoors, always avoid overwatering the plant as it can easily slowdown its growth rate.
There are many species of the female marijuana seeds available in the market. Some of these seeds are large and hard thus requiring a longer germination period. However, most seeds are soft and take a very short time to germinate.

Before planting your seeds, one thing you need to avoid is pre-soaking your seeds in water or wet paper. This is because fresh seeds contain a healthy embryo with a lot of water inside. Subjecting the seed to excess water leads to tissue rot and loss of oxygen.

The right procedure to follow when germinating the marijuana seedling is to use nutritious soil filled in a small container (preferably 8—10cm in diameter). Dig a small hole at the center of the container (1.5cm) deep then place your seedling in a horizontal position. Always use chlorine free water and always maintain a pH level of 6—6.5. Use a calibrated beaker when watering your seedling to avoid overwatering and maintain consistent temperatures of 25°C or 77°F.

Rockwool can also be used in the early stages of your marijuana seeds. Made from mineral fibers, Rockwool holds moisture and provides enough oxygen for your seeds' life. Use Rockwool cubes of about 1×1 inches, soak them in water then place your seedlings inside. Cover the top with more Rockwool then place them in a tray. Ensure that the location is warm enough (about 22°C or 74°F) for an accelerated germination process.

Please only use this if you have Rockwool laying around because it takes a long time to breakdown in nature and has a slightly high Ph.

Instead use starter cubes and seedling plugs for germination. If the seed is in the hole simply pinch the top gently to seal it.

Seedling plugs (do a search for rapid rooter on amazon)

The seed that sprouts splits into two halves releasing the tail and the husk. The tail grows long and penetrates down below the soil to supply enough water and nutrients to raise the stalk. Within a few days, the stalk becomes stronger and holds the two seed halves high above the ground. The seed halves act as panels for trapping energy which is essential for the marijuana's chlorophyll production while the taproot develops a network of hair-like roots which gather more nutrients and strengthen the plant's grip to the ground. If you see the plant coming out of the seed, it's time to put them into the final (big) plant pot.

10 days after the seed has split into two, the first two leaves of the marijuana plant develop in the middle of the seed. These leaves are known as sucker leaves and they mark the beginning of your marijuana leaf growth. After another few days, more leaves will appear with two lobes, three lobes, five lobes and finally the famous seven lobes leaves will appear. At this time, your marijuana plant will take its initial shape and everyone will be able to recognize the plant.

A seed with two additional leaves

The seeding stage mostly goes for a period between 3--6 weeks. During this stage, your marijuana plant needs to stay healthy to pave way for a productive vegetative stage.

During the seeding stage, your marijuana plant requires stable temperatures of between 70--85°F (20-30°C). If it's too hot, you can always move the light higher or closer in case it's too cold. You can identify whether or not your seedlings are experiencing too much heat by looking at the leaves as they tend curl upwards. These symptoms are also visible when your plant is not receiving enough water.

Leaves are curling up because it's too hot

When growing marijuana at home, light is another factor that needs to be observed at all cost. Seeds grown outdoors enjoy as much sunlight as possible thus boosting their growth. Therefore, to maintain the consistency, your marijuana seedling should be exposed to as much light as possible. Fluorescent lights are the best to consider as they don't consume a lot of power and don't emit much heat. Place the fluorescent lights close enough to the seedlings at a distance of about 2-3 inches (5-7,5 cm).

When growing your marijuana indoors, always remember that every plant has a *"light saturation point"*. This is a point whereby your plant receives more light than it really needs. At this point, your marijuana reduces its growth rate since there's no point of growing too fast when the amount of light is more than enough. Therefore, it's important to check the amount of light being exposed to the seedlings and make sure its moderate to suit each plant.

Pre-flowering

The pre-flowering stage of a marijuana plant is a very crucial stage as your plant will definitely start showing signs of maturity. Also referred to as the pre-adult stage, your marijuana now concentrates more on developing to reproduce. One way of ensuring that your cannabis plant undergoes a successful pre-flowering period is to reduce the amount of light from the initial 24/0 day/night photo period to 12/12 day/night light period.

The pre-flowering stage of the marijuana plant starts 4-6 weeks after the vegetative period. Unless you're very observant or if you use a magnifying glass, it's very hard to tell if a marijuana plant is pre-flowering. However, for those informed farmers, you can easily bet on whether a plant is male or female just by observing its characteristics. One way to tell the gender is through observing the pre-flowers. Also, the male tend to mature much faster than the female marijuana plants.
The male pre-flower of a cannabis plant mostly takes the shape of a "*spade*" like the one in a deck of cards. During the final stage, these stipules grow into pollen sacs which look like grapes. At the final stage, these sacs burst open and releases pollen grains to the female cannabis plants.

On the other hand, the female cannabis has longer and narrower stipules with a fatter base. Sometimes, the stipules may be longer with white hairs (pistils) at the tip or shorter but not rounded like a male pre-flower.

Always introduce your marijuana strains to the flowering stage after the pre-flowering period has shown up to avoid interrupting with the cannabis growth. Introducing your plant to 12 hours of light and 12 hours of darkness earlier than expected may stress the plant causing an abnormal growth which may results to your marijuana being hermaphrodites (both male and female flowers).

Flowering stage

The flowering stage of the marijuana plant is the most important to most farmers. The last three weeks of this stage means that your plant will explosively produce more flowers and buds, especially when the lighting is adjusted to 12 hours during the day and 12 hours in the night. The buds keep on swelling while the cannabis plant takes its initial odor. At this stage, keen farmers will start seeing sticky resin on the leaves of the marijuana plant. This resin is mostly concentrated on the buds and is the most crucial end ingredient in the cannabis plant as it contains the highest percentage of THC.

Sticky THC on a plant

Depending with the growing environment which includes the nutrients levels, the fertilizers used and the temperatures, the flowering period usually take between 6—10 weeks.

During the flowering stage of the marijuana plant, growers are free to administer grow or bloom fertilizers. These fertilizers are usually applied during the first or second week of the flowering stage to bolster the plant's growth. For instance, if you want your cannabis plant to grow taller, you can administer grow fertilizer. If the marijuana already has the right size or if you don't need taller plants due to space issues, you can give them bloom fertilizer. Note that, the reason why you should administer bloom fertilizer to your cannabis plants is due to its 13/14 PK mixture (popular fertilizer). This means that your plant is fed with the right mixture of phosphorus and potassium which assists in the flowering process.

Foliar feeding is the next possible step to take after fertilizing your marijuana plant. Administering foliar to your marijuana supplies enough nutrients to the plant which can help correct any nutritional deficiencies. When growing indoors, add the foliar feeding about half an hour before lighting the lamps to avoid burning the leaves when wet. Spray your marijuana plants with foliar feeding twice or thrice every week. Pay a closer look every time you spray to discover which nutrients the plants need.

lemon kush day 105

During the flowering stage, always maintain a temperature consistency of between 68—77°F (20--25°C), humidity of between 50—70% and a light cycle of 12 hours. During this stage, avoid interrupting or confusing your plant in any way. Observe the temperature, humidity and nutrients consistency to avoid backsliding your plant's growth cycle.

About a month after the flowering stage has begun, your marijuana plant will stop producing leaves and instead start developing flowers and buds. The leaves will be covered with transparent resin which with time will darken and produce a very strong odor. With time, the marijuana plant will grow wider and close together while the buds will expand. Due to the weight of the plant, you'll be required to use sticks or cordage to support the plant as it matures.

Two weeks after your cannabis has fully matured, you should stop fertilizing the plants. You can identify the plant's maturity through observing the leaves (turns yellow), the odor (very concentrated), transparent resin on the leaves, the pistils (turns brown) and the overall weight of the plant. After you've seized spraying the plant with fertilizer, only concentrate on irrigating the cannabis for the rest of the time to rinse away minerals and nutrients for safe human consumption.

Harvest time

When is my marijuana plant ready for harvest? This is one of the burning questions most cannabis farmers ask themselves immediately after their plants reach the flowering stage. As one of the most anticipated moments in the life of a marijuana plant, harvest time varies depending with the type of strains and the environment (indoors or outdoors).

There are various ways farmers can determine whether the cannabis plant is ready for harvest. One way is to look at the calyxes. During the final stages, these calyxes swell and ripen producing a layer of glass like resin on the surface. Another method you can use to determine harvest time for a cannabis plant is checking the ration of red to white on the pistils. Let's review these methods more broadly to give you more information on how to precisely identify when your marijuana is ready for harvest.

The pistil method

During the flowering stage, the pistils on the buds of your marijuana plant are mostly sticky and white. These signs mean that your plant is not yet ready for harvest and needs more time. When using a magnifying glass, you'll notice that most pistils are white and just a few are red/brown. When the plant is ready for harvest, about 70% of the pistils will turn red/brown meaning they've achieved their highest THC levels. Note that, if you delay to harvest the plants, the strong effects of the THC will convert to a more relaxing CBN.

However, the pistil method is not 100% reliable as some strains may not reveal maturity just by observing the color of the pistils. In such an occasion, the next method will be much more reliable.

Trichome method

This method is the most precise and involves checking the cannabis resin/trichome using a magnifying glass. Trichome is a sticky frosty substance that appears on the surface of the leaves and buds. When ready for harvest, the resin looks like small mushrooms with a ball at the top. The small balls contain THC and at this time, the marijuana plant is ready for harvest.

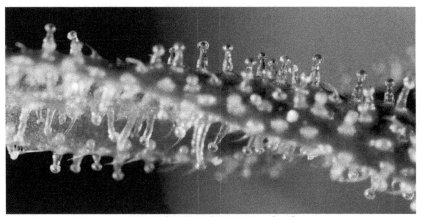

The Trichome method
Image credits: cannabisculture.com

Check your seeds' harvest date

The last method a farmer can rely on when determining the best time for harvesting marijuana is to check the harvest date as indicated on the sachets. Although this method can be worth considering, the results are merely orientative since the flowering and the harvest period depends on several factors such as the growing conditions (indoors or outdoors), types of fertilizers used and the latitudes.

Example of a growing process

Evolution of the plant

The following images are an example of a growing process with a cloned stem. Plants have been cloned 20 days prior to start. This is to give you an idea of what to expect when growing your own plants.

To recap these are the stages a plant goes through:

- Seedling – 7 days
- pre-flowering or vegetative – 2 to 3 weeks
- flowering – 6 to 8 weeks

Generally, we are talking about 2-4 months depending on the installation you have and the kind of plant.

After the flowering stage (read about this in the flowering stage chapter) it's time for harvest. It will take 3 to 10 days for your harvest to dry out.

Cloned Lemon kush day 1 (after germination)

Plants after day 10

Day 28

Day 40

Day 71

Day 105

Day 115: harvest time

Drying

4. Plant health

The health of the cannabis plant starts right from the seedling stage. For the seeds to germinate properly, they need to be moistened and planted in nutritious and well-drained soil. When your seedlings pop their heads up from the soil, adjust the lights and the temperatures to achieve an average of 72°F (22°C) for 24 hours. During this stage, your marijuana plant needs a reliable climate to develop steady roots and leaves. In this chapter, we will concentrate on the most important measures which every cannabis farmer should focus on when growing healthy cannabis plants.

Pest control

Cannabis is a flowering plant that grows annually from April through September. The plant can either be male or female with the female being the one responsible for flowering and producing buds. Just like other flowering plants, cannabis is susceptible to pests and diseases. Therefore, it's important for growers to always countercheck their plants for signs of holes, insects or spots on the surface of the leaves.

Incase these bugs/pests have already affected your marijuana plants; the only choice you've got is to spray an insecticide which will eliminate them without affecting your health. In this case, use pesticides marked "*safe to use on food crops*" as cannabis is regarded as a food crop just like fruits or veggies. Although cannabis is known to be a pest resistant plant, there are a few bugs and infections which can fatally affect it such as thrips, white flies, botrytis, red spider mites and caterpillars.

There are three steps involved when it comes to protecting your marijuana strains from pests. They are; prevention, identification, management and eradication. Let's examine each of these pests and suggest necessary measures to bring them down. Note that, although there are many types of pests/bugs associated with marijuana, we will only look at the most common when growing your stains indoors.

- **Spider mites**: these are the most common pests that attack the marijuana plants grown in indoor tents. They mostly attack the plant during optimal growth and survive well on high temperatures, low humidity and poorly ventilated areas. When your marijuana is under attack by spider mites, you'll see tiny yellow dots both on the surface and underneath the leaves.

Signs of spider mites

- **Aphids**: these pests are very dangerous when they attack your marijuana. They can damage the plant or even expose your marijuana to severe viruses and diseases. Aphids are mostly found on the stems and lower parts of the leaves where they suck sap from the plant.

Aphids on marijuana

- **Thrips**: these pests are also very common in indoor cannabis farming. The *Frankliniella Occidentalis* is a common species of the thrips that attacks the marijuana plant. These pests are mostly found on the lower parts of the leaves and mostly leave silver stains or black dots on the surface of the leaves.

A leave with Thrips

- **Sciarid flies**: also known as *Sciaridae*, these pests are common in cannabis plants and are mostly found in wet and low light intensity environments. These insects are small and mostly attack the root system. The only way to combat these insects is by reducing the irrigation frequency or using mulching.

Development of Sciarid flies (fruit flies)

Fertilizing

The type of fertilizer you choose to administer to your marijuana plant will directly impact the growth of your plant throughout its life cycle. There are different types of fertilizers one can rely on when growing marijuana. You can either buy from your local garden store or mix certain ingredients to make your own organic fertilizer.

Depending with your experience for growing cannabis, you can either buy professional fertilizers which have already been mixed with the correct ratios or you can simply buy different ingredients and mix them yourself. However, before deciding on the type of fertilizer to use, you first need to know to growing medium of your cannabis (depending with the available space) and the technique you'll use to grow the strains whether soil, hydroponics. With the right watering techniques and the right amounts of nutrients in the soil, these fertilizers will work well for your marijuana strains that grow in soil or hydroponics.

Marijuana booster

This type of fertilizer is the best to consider when you want your plant to induce all the necessary nutrients. For your marijuana to develop strong roots and vibrant flowers/leaves, it needs a mixture of phosphorus, nitrogen and potassium. Since you're growing your marijuana indoors, give them a 20% balance of these three ingredients immediately they start the leafing stage. Remember to dilute the formula as listed on the package to avoid overdosing your marijuana strains which may lead to shock.

Fox Farms Trio

A top pick by most newbie marijuana farmers, Fox Farms Trio is the best way to go if you really need to achieve higher yields. There are various versions of these fertilizers available ranging from hydroponics, soil versions and coco coir versions. When using Fox Farms fertilizers, you'll receive three bottles containing *"Grow Big"*, *"Tiger Bloom"* and *"Big Bloom"* fertilizers.

Dyna-Gro

New marijuana farmers looking forward to purchase strong but cost effective fertilizers should check the foliage-pro and bloom fertilizers from Dyna-Gro. These fertilizers can be used in any cannabis growing method ranging from hydro, soil to coco coir. These fertilizers can be used throughout the growing cycle of the cannabis plant. However, for higher results, the Foliage-Pro can be used during the vegetative stage while the Bloom can be administered during the flowering stage of the marijuana plant.

General Hydroponics Flora Series Nutrient Trio

Hydroponics fertilizer is the best for beginners and advanced growers. It comes with a performance kit to check the pH levels as well as everything you need to apply during the entire growth cycle of the marijuana. This fertilizer can be used in coco coir method, soil and hydroponics method as well and is the best for marijuana farming.

Watering

Marijuana is a resilient plant which means it can tolerate basic mistakes to some extent. However, if the plant induces nutrients and water in wrong quantities for a long time, it can develop deep-rooted problems which can be fatal in the end. Cannabis plants need a lot of water to produce healthy leaves and buds. Water is the most essential aspect of the plant's growth and is used in all the marijuana life stages starting from photosynthesis, transpiration, nutrients intake and leaves formation. So, if water is so paramount to the growth of your cannabis, how do I water my strains?

Unless you're living near a natural source of water like a mountainous stream, most of us use water supplied by the county council. Most of this water contains substantial amounts of chlorine which is only good for human consumption and not for farming. Therefore, before using tap water to grow your cannabis, you need to find ways of lowering the high chlorine levels to avoid shocking your cannabis strains. Before watering your marijuana plants, allow the water to stand for a day or two in an open container. This lowers the level of chlorine in the water and also allows the water to achieve room temperature.

Under-watering

Under-watering happens when your marijuana plant is deprived off water at any stage during its life cycle. Since marijuana is a semi-arid plant, it needs a little dry period for an accelerated growth. However, this period should not take long as your plant will need abundant water for nutrients induction. One common symptom of under watered marijuana strains is wilting leaves. Wilting is caused by lack of enough water in the leaves cells causing them to shrink and therefore bend the entire leaf. To fix this problem, simply supply your marijuana plant with enough water and the leaves will slowly strengthen back and photosynthesize.

A marijuana plant that needs some more water

Over-watering

This is one of the common mistakes newbie marijuana growers make. Giving your plants a lot of water will slowly introduce molds and fungus in the root system as well as lower the growth of your strains. This condition may lead to pythium (root rot), powdery mildew, botrytis (grey mold) and oxygenless (a severe soil condition). The first sign of overwatering growers see is yellowing of the leaf tips. Although this condition is mostly mistaken for nutrient deficiency, leaving the plants to dry for some time is the first process of curing this condition. This is how you should water your marijuana plant from its initial stage to the final flowering stage.

- **Seedling** - during the seedling phase of the cannabis life cycle, the soil needs to be moist and the little seedling needs to be watered moderately at list twice a day. Use a hand sprayer when watering the little sprout and avoid spraying the water directly to the fragile stem as it can bend or break easily.

- **Vegetative** - the auto flowering stage of the cannabis growth needs a lot of water. At this stage, you'll need to water your plants regularly regardless of the size of your container. Always check the first few centimeters of the soil if it's dry or wet. If it's dry, that means it's time to water your plants. You can also lift the container up to feel the weight of the soil. If the container is light, it means the soil is dry and if it's heavy, it means the soil is wet.

- **Flowering** - similar to the vegetative stage, the flowering stage requires you to water your marijuana strains more regularly as the plants tend to chew more water at this stage than ever. Always check the soil before watering to ensure that you give the plants enough water dosage to avoid over-watering. Usually at this stage, the cannabis plants induce more water for flower/bud formation while another small portion of water evaporates due to high temperatures.

Overwatering (leaves begin to become brown from the tip to the stem)

Controlling temperature

Temperature is one of the fundamental aspects that determine whether your cannabis will boom or not. When growing marijuana at home, you need to maintain a moderate temperature ranging from 70-85°F (20-30°C). The temperatures in your marijuana grow room depends on several factors. They include the location of your room, the number of strains, the types/number of lights in the room and the size of the room. When the lights are on, the temperatures should range between 68°F-77°F (20°C-25°C). However, as the plants grow older, the temperature will need to increase to a maximum of 80°F (27°C). When the lights are off, the temperatures should slightly lower with a 5°C difference to range at 62°F-72°F (17°C-22°C).

You can measure the temperatures of your grow room using an analog or digital thermometer. A digital thermometer is ideal as it can recall the previous temperatures recorded. When measuring the temperatures, always move to various spots within the room. Some people install several fans throughout the room for uniform airflow.

How to lower the room temperature
Depending with the lights we use and the size of the growing room, temperatures can sometimes increase to as high as 122°F (50°C). With such high temperatures, your marijuana plants can be fatally affected leading to low production. To lower the temperatures, always light up the grow room a few hours after sunset and a few hours after sunrise. This way, your marijuana will enjoy light during the coolest hours and enjoy moderate temperatures during the day when it's hot outside.

How to increase the temperature

When growing cannabis in cold areas, temperatures in the inside need to be high at all times to avoid shocking your strains. You can use swivel fans as a means of distributing heat throughout the room or you can install stronger lamps in every corner of the grow room. If the temperatures outside are below freezing point, a heater or a radiator with a thermostat will be handy and easy to work with.

Using Artificial lights

Best light spectrum for growth

Growing marijuana indoors has numerous advantages and disadvantages. There are lots of factors you need to consider when setting up your grow room to avoid any errors. One of these factors is the type of lights you'll need to use during the different stages of the marijuana life cycle.

The first stage (vegetative) of the marijuana life cycle goes for a period of one week to 40 days depending on the type of seed that's planted. During this stage, a standard light cycle of 18 hours day and 6 hours night will have to be adapted for effective results. Experienced growers prefer 24 hours of the lighting cycle during this stage for quicker and accelerated growth.

The next stage (flowering) requires a light cycle of 12 hours day and 12 hours night to allow the marijuana to flower and produce buds. Always be careful when introducing your marijuana strains to the flowering stage. Although it mostly takes about 40 days to achieve this stage, it's wise to check the overall height and health of the cannabis first.

During the vegetative stage, your marijuana plant will most likely prefer fluorescent bulbs as they produce tons of blue light spectrums that are beneficially to your plant. The best thing about fluorescent lights is that they're cheap and produce less heat. However, as your marijuana progresses to the flowering stage, High Pressure Sodium lights will the best to consider as they'll only be on for 12 hours as compared to the previous 24 hours. In addition to this, HPS lights produce red/orange lights which tend to stimulate the cannabis hormones leading to flowering/buds production.

High Intensity Discharge Lights (HID)

There are different lights you can use during the growing process of the cannabis plant. However, every type of lighting you introduce to your plants must suit a particular growth stage as this will impact your cannabis strains at the final stage. Some of the best lights that perform perfectly well in the growth cycle of the cannabis are the High Intensity Discharge lights. These lights are relatively cheaper as compared to LED lights and are the best to consider throughout the life cycle of the marijuana. There are three types of HID lights in the market which include the High Pressure Sodium (HPS), the Metal Halide (MH) and the Mercury Vapor (MV) lights.

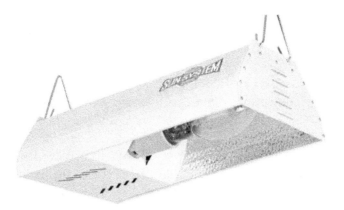

HID Light

Metal Halide Systems (MH)

Majority of the Metal Halide lights produce light in a blue spectrum which is paramount during the vegetative stage. This is because the lights tend to replicate the natural sunlight during summer seasons. These lights encourage healthy growth of your cannabis especially the stem, the leaves and the branches leading to shorter and bushy strains. Although MH lights are among the best known lights for indoor marijuana growth, it's not recommended to use them throughout the life cycle.

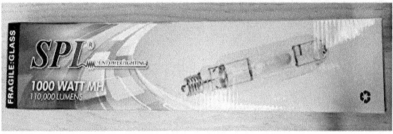

Metal Halide light

High Pressure Sodium systems (HPS)

When your marijuana achieves the flowering stage, growers are recommended to switch to the HPS lights. This is because; HPS lights emit yellow, orange and red light spectrums which triggers the productive stage of the marijuana growth. The reason why HPS lights are used in the flowering and not the vegetative stage is because they deliver skinny and tall strains unlike the MH lights which deliver short and bushy cannabis plants. One drawback with the HPS lights is that they create more heat which consumes a lot of electricity. You also need to have an air conditioner and a fan for uniform air circulation throughout the grow room.

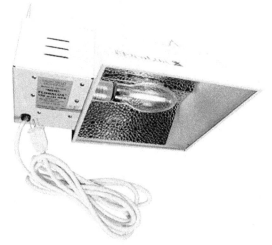

High pressure sodium light

Fluorescent lights

Coated with phosphor and filled with a mixture of different gases, fluorescent lights can be used in the growth cycle of the cannabis plant. These lights come in a range of different sizes (from 6--96 inches) and wattage (from 4--214 watts). Fluorescent lights are known for releasing low amounts of heat in a grow room and therefore you'll need to place them close enough to the plants for perfect results. One advantage with these lights is that they're cheap and they consume less power. On the other hand, due to their low light intensity, your plants will produce less buds/flowers in the final stage leading to lower yields. Therefore, for perfect results, most farmers opt to replace them with HID lights or the expensive T5 fluorescent lights.

Fluorescent light

LED grow lights

In the past, cannabis farmers used MH and HPS lights for indoor use during the vegetative and the flowering stages of the cannabis life cycle. Although these lights works perfectly well, they have been facing a major drawback of high power consumption. In addition to this, these bulbs lose their effectiveness quite fast reducing the amount of light and consequently forcing the marijuana strains to work extra harder to get sufficient light.

To solve this problem, farmers have turned to the use of LED lights which have proved to work well than both MH and HPS lights. LED lights come in a variety of options that can be used in different stages of the cannabis growth cycle. In case of the vegetative cycle, you only need to purchase LED that emits blue lights while in the flowering stage; you'll need to get those with red/orange lights. The best thing about LED lights is that they consume 60%-90% less power than HID lights.

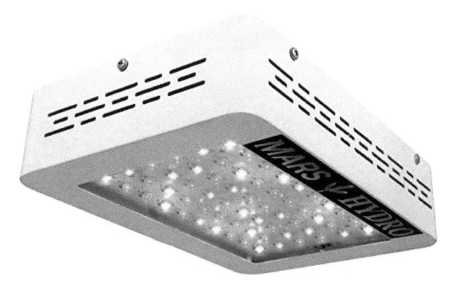

Led grow light

Light reflection

As you all know, light is very important for the growth and production of a cannabis plant. For your strains to flower and produce more buds, they need enough light and heat throughout the process. Depending with the size of the grow room and the type of lighting used, marijuana strains can either flourish or slow down the growth rate. Due to this reason, we've compiled various reflectivity options which growers can check on depending with their personal setup and the budget.

Grow tent walls (99% light reflectivity)

Grow tent walls provide the best cannabis growing environment of any option. Available in different sizes to suit the number of your strains, these light reflecting tent walls are water resilient and easy to clean making them the number one choice in the market.

A grow tent

Panda Plastics (95% light reflectivity)

Also referred to as black and white polymer, panda plastics can be used to trap enough light for your plant's growth. Simply nail the polymer on the wall with the white side facing the light while the black side is at the back. Although they're quite expensive, panda plastics help trap enough light for your marijuana growth.

Mylar (95% light reflectivity)
Mylar is another reflective material that comes in rolls or small sheets. There are two common versions of this material which include Foylon and C3 anti-detection film. Mylar is hard to clean and needs replacement after every few grows. Although it's translucent, it does retain enough heat in the grow room which is essential for the growth of your marijuana. You might recognize this because it's used for emergency situations where they wrap this foil around people to get them warm.

Orca Grow Film (94% light reflectivity)

The Orca Glow Film uses a unique structure that resembles the skin of a killer whale. Although it's quite expensive, this film is mold resistant, thick and easy to clean. Similar to the panda film, the Orca Grow Film requires you to face the white side towards the plants while the black part faces outwards.

Apart from these reflectivity options, there are other alternatives growers can always consider when looking for quality light reflectors for your grow room. They include; mirrors, Styrofoam (70% reflectivity), white poster board (60% reflectivity), aluminum foil (60% reflectivity), emergency blankets (70% reflectivity) and Kool Seal Elastomeric Roof Coating (90% reflectivity).

Ventilation

Apart from maintaining the correct temperatures inside your grow rooms, there are other parameters you need to keep into account such as installing perfect ventilation systems. With proper ventilation, your marijuana strains have the freedom to perform all the necessary gas exchanges and heat evacuation to achieve perfect climate for healthy growth. With that in mind, this section will review different cooling systems available and how to use them in order to maintain cool temperatures inside the grow rooms.

Extractor fan system

These fans are very essential in a marijuana grow room as they help to pull hot air out and replace it with cool fresh air. These fans are mostly strong as they have to suck all the hot air inside the room and uniformly release cool air from the outside. Extractor fans come in different sizes which suit different grow rooms. For instance, a 23"×23" grow room requires a 4 inch exhaust fan and controller. On the other hand, a 40"×40" grow room requires a 6 inch fan for perfect results.

Oscillating fans

This is another fan system you can use to keep your marijuana plants cool and healthy. Apart from using the extractor fan, cannabis growers can use oscillating fans to blow cool air between the plants and maintain cool temperatures.

Using a dehumidifier

Apart from enhancing good air circulation, humidity control is another aspect you must never forget to consider. Usually when growing indoors, humidity buildup must be present. There are plenty of diseases that may affect your plants in such a condition and this may greatly impact the growth of your cannabis. Therefore using a dehumidifier allows you to eliminate excess humidity from the grow room.

Note that, excess humidity lowers resin production at the flowering stage of the cannabis growth cycle. For perfect results, ensure that humidity remains at 80-90% during the cloning stage, 60-70% during the vegetative stage and 40-60% during the flowering stage. I recommend getting your dehumidifier and humidity sensor from eBay or amazon.

Cheap $45 dehumidifier (amazon)

5. Extra

Hiding your plants from the outside world

Depending with your state laws, growing cannabis might turn to be an illegal business that can send you behind bars if you're not careful. There are many benefits which come with growing cannabis indoors and outdoors. However, when it comes to stealth, indoor growing becomes the best method to consider. All in all, we will review some of the many different ways you can grow marijuana both indoors and outdoors and never get caught by the authorities.

Don't be this guy

When growing indoors

Smell: during the vegetative stage of your marijuana growth, the strains tend to make a clean faint smell that's hard to distinguish. However, as it approaches the flowering stage, the smell changes leaving everyone asking *"What's that smell?"* Therefore, to deal with the issue of odor, you'll need to install carbon filters or odor neutralizers in your grow room to suck or neutralize the cannabis smell preventing it from going into your living room.

Sound: buying low quality electrical equipment such as fans, air pumps or lights can produce a lot of noise that can leak multiple walls thus raising questions. To avoid this problem, buy high quality fans which are less powerful and less noisy when operating. Hung the exhaust fans inside the tent with ropes, ensure that the air intake holes are large enough and be aware of exactly where the noise is going.

Sight: your outside appearance to the public tells more about you. When growing cannabis, ensure that you stay decent so that anyone who sees you doing growing related activities may not get suspicious of you. To maintain high quality decency:

- Always move your equipment at night

- Always check the kind of garbage you through away in your garbage can.

- Always walk around your house/compound on different times of the day to ensure that nothing stands out as suspicious.

- Maintain a good relationship with your neighbors as they're the first people to report you in case they notice questionable activities going on.

When growing outdoors

Although outdoor growing results in healthy marijuana strains in the long run, it's very difficult to maintain stealth. However, there are a number of methods you can rely on to hide your strains from the authorities or nosy neighbors.

- Plant your marijuana next to trees and bushes in locations where other people can't notice. Once your secret spot is discovered do not go back to recover your harvest because the authorities may have setup a camera trap.

- Try and change the disguise of your plants as much as possible. Some people can prune the leaves to give them another shape while other may pin different flowers on the cannabis to help in the disguise.

- Finally, plant the cannabis strains between other weeds that look exactly the same in terms of color, size and shape. This method creates a kind of camouflage to your marijuana making it difficult to distinguish at first sight.

Cloning your marijuana plants

What's a cannabis clone and what are the advantages of doing it? Well, to begin with, cloning of cannabis strains is one of the easiest and fastest ways of multiplying your marijuana plants without worrying on gender. A clone is a small piece of plant that has been extracted or cut from the original mother plant. Clones are usually pure copies of the original mother plant and usually contain the same genes and characteristics as the parent. Cloning is a smart way of propagating a cannabis plant without worrying on gender. If you notice that your cannabis is among the best in the market or maybe it's resilient to some pests or environmental conditions, you can simply clone them to produce multiple "copies". With that being said, we will focus on some effective techniques you can use to clone healthy and perfect marijuana plants.

How to clone a cannabis plant

The first step to take when cloning a marijuana plant is disinfecting all your tools such as scissors/razors and getting everything ready for the "operation". Look for strains that show pure signs of maturity and good health before cutting preferably new strains. To detect mature strains, always check on the leaves/nodes connection (the leaves/nodes should be alternating and shouldn't be connected at the same exact point on the stem).

When cutting, choose a spot where there's a fresh growing stem and cut at an angle of 45°. Ensure that the new cutting is about 5-8 inches for more desirable results. Some people may choose to split the bottom of their cutting or scrap it a bit to expose more of the inside. This idea is perfect as it promotes faster rooting.

After you've cut your clone, trim the lower leaves and soak it in water so it can develop roots by itself. In case the leaves are not trimmed, your clone may focus more on making leaves grow instead of focusing on developing roots. Some growers prefer to induce rooting hormones for faster root growth. This can be done through dipping the freshly cut stems into a gel or rooting hormone powder.

Roots developing on a clone

Now that you have the clones ready, a wise grower will place them inside a humidity dome, a heating pad or an automatic cloner. Usually, new clones require weak light and warm temperatures to develop roots faster. Therefore, you should expose them to temperatures ranging from 72-77°F (22-25°C) and an 18/6 night/dark cycle for the first 10 days. Depending with the parent plant, cannabis clones may take 7 days to 2 weeks to fully develop a strong rooting system. Always be patient and wait until the roots are fully formed to transplant your marijuana plants.

Final words

I hope you found this book helpful. You should know now how to start growing your own marijuana at home. There are a lot of factors that are not discussed in this book because I wanted it to keep it short and powerful so you can get a general idea of how it works and the work that comes with it.

If you're keen on setting up your own cannabis plants indoors you should do some more research yourself on forums.
If you got some time in your schedule, would you please give this book a rating on amazon? This really helps me out.

Thanks for reading my book and let's grow these plants!
Regards,
Addison Edge & Gene Guzman

CPSIA information can be obtained
at www.ICGtesting.com
Printed in the USA
LVHW022056231118
598038LV00024B/641/P